Any Day Now

Geoffrey J Fox

PublishAmerica

Baltimore

First printing

All names and events were created in the mind of the author

ISBN: 1-4137-1412-9
PUBLISHED BY PUBLISHAMERICA, LLLP
www.publishamerica.com
Baltimore

Printed in the United States of America

To Joy

We all have a hero
one we wish we could be
Mine is my sister
she's a hero tc me...

Table of Poems

<u>Rhyming Couplets and Free Rhyme</u>

Free Verse

Locked

I try to open the door but my hand is not the key
The redundant questions seem to be mocking me
A gentle breeze whistles past my ear
The long walk is only a third complete
The waves crash with anger in the endless ocean
Time is crucial
My veins are starved
Home isn't here, perhaps it's through the door
No, I must remember this is my home
I leave you with my gun
Please still be you when I return
My body aches
His life depends on me
Our lives depend on him
The sand is still warm
I kiss your dark skin
My mission continues

Bench

I sit on this familiar bench
and feel a whirlwind of emotion
I look back on the 23 years of
memory this bench represents
As a boy I would sit here
and dream of being a man
As a man I sit here
and dream of being a boy
Neighborhood get togethers
took place in this park and I remember
sitting here laughing with the neighborhood kids
while our parents talked about whatever it was
grownups talked of
My best friend and I would
let the sun dry us from this bench
after morning swims
the summer before we started high school
I've unleashed my dog present
and dog past and watched from this bench
as they ran through the park with reckless abandon
after bugs and scary shadows
This bench has watched me grow
as it has remained the same
And as I grow
coming back here always
brings me to a place where time has no meaning
and worry is just a word

Visitor

I'm awoken by a gentle rapping at the front of my
brain
It's the visitor who used to come around quite a bit
He's not graced me with his presence for as long as I
can recall
His lack of attendance has been noted and has been
greatly missed
It's been so long I don't recognize him at first glance
He turns to leave just as I realize who he is and invite
him in
He accepts the invitation graciously
When I ask to take his coat, he declines and states,
"this won't be a long visit"
We share a cup of coffee and the morning together
Then from the dirt covered window in my brain, I
watch "Happiness" leave once again

Incomplete

Broken promises
Insecurities
Another day of tears
Her hand slips out of mine
Nothing is the same
Incomplete
A single purpose
Mind in rewind
Silent screams
Empty nights
Painful scars
Promises broken

It's Over

I never let what happened stay in the past
It's so hard but you're leaving
No one else is around
You do something to me that I can't explain
You left enchanted
Look at the stars
Can you even hear me?
I watch you float away
I promised that I'd run away with you
Just try your best
My soul's escaping
You're all that I want
I'm so glad that you fell in love with me
It's over

Time

This fire won't heat the never-ending chill
This smile won't hide the never-ending pain
This money won't cease the never-ending greed
These people won't halt the never-ending loneliness
These pills won't end the never-ending numbness
These screams won't stop the never-ending silence
This knowledge won't change the never-ending
ignorance
Only time will terminate this never-ending life

I Remember

I remember the scent of alcohol and cigarettes
Your inability to express love
The countless glares across the kitchen table
The fear for my safety

I remember the birthdays forgotten
The lack of support in my academic achievements
The absence at the ballpark when I hit my first home
run
The rage within

I remember praying to never be like you
To show *my* son love
To take *my* daughter shopping
To give *my* wife a life worth living

Someday I hope to remember the day things
changed
The day the scent of alcohol disappeared
The day you showed forgiveness for the damage
done
Most importantly the day you decided to love me

Different

The morning light creaked in through the blinds
Something's different
The dog is still snoring in the corner of the room
The dirty walls are covered in the usual nicotine and
finger prints
The house remains empty…as do I
There's a difference
It's just unseen
A tear rolls over my lip and onto my tongue
A smile fills my face
The visitor has returned

Coffee

Coffee and the night
Conversations over candle light
Her gentle words laughing in my ear
Friendship on the verge of more
Smiles that begin where others end
Desire growing like wildfire
Two hearts with one goal
Like into love
Coffee and the night

7:13 P.M.

I look at my watch and a smile fills my face
I sip the sweet lemonade and put my legs up
The breeze brings the salty scent of the ocean
The sky begins to change colors
The blues melt into pink
The ocean begins to engulf the sun
The water appears to be aflame with desire
The two old friends meet again

2 Miles

The stars fill the sky
The full moon warns us to go home
Driving with no expectations, but in search of
something
Something better than this
The east brings heartbreak
The west brings betrayal
The north brings loneliness
The south brings promise
Promise is enticing
Desire fills the car
The rolling hills occupy the rearview mirror
The road narrows
The street sign reads, "Hope-2 Miles"

Letter to Lost Love

Dearest past,

My soul has been calling on you this gloomy morn. I felt you in my sleep last eve. Could that have been genuine? Perhaps you felt me with you? My thoughts and my actions still to this day have never betrayed thee. I know better than to think the same is true in you. For your thoughts betrayed us both while we were still in bliss. I want you to know my heart still beats your name and my lungs still breathe your life. I hurt for you and I love you.

Always,

Broke Hart

Pool

Life is a game of 8-ball
Rack em up and I'll explain
Ok, we start with this cue ball representing your life
The balls racked being your decisions in life
and the 8 ball representing death
Now break em up
"Break"
Good break, you knocked in a solid
So solids now represent your path in life...your goals
Stripes being the obstacles
It's your shot sport
"Crash"
See there, you just knocked in a stripe on accident
Perhaps that represents an affair or a dabble into
drugs
something that's holding you back from your goals
See, what I'm trying to tell you is simple
Like life, the object of 8-ball is to get all your goals met
without any of lives little obstacles
then you die a winner
Get it?

Greyhound

I begin eating my lunch on Main Street at an outdoor
deli
I look around and take in another perfect Michigan
fall day, as I notice a beautiful woman
She is sitting on a bench across the street under the
Greyhound sign
I watch as she removes a book from her purse and
begins reading
David Copperfield, my fathers favorite
A strand of her long blonde hair falls out of place
and she makes no effort to put it back
I shut my eyes and am instantly overtaken by a vision
of "us" together
hand in hand smiling by a pool
We are watching a little girl swim
Our little girl!
The little girl is beautiful with her mom's blonde hair
and my green eyes
The little girl runs out of the pool and over to me,
giving me a huge wet hug saying,
"I love you daddy"
I hug her back and fill with happiness, a happiness
foreign to me
Perhaps a reverie sent by fate?
I get up to go talk to her as I open my eyes
She is gone
I watch as the Greyhound pulls away

Rain

The rain continues to fall
Eight days straight
Washing away the past
Helping to grow new life
I can sense the rain beginning to halt
Smiles fill the breeze
Life begins sprouting from the damp earth
A chill slowly rips a path down my back
as a bird begins singing somewhere to the west
The sun shows its face
I feel promise begin to take root
Where have you been?

You Can't

You can't be loved without loving
You can't grow without critique
You can't be rejected without an attempt
You can't change without a little help
You can't win without once losing
You can't beat the odds without trying
You can't appreciate the good without the bad
You can't truly live without risk

Few Days

You said it'd only be a few days
then you'd return to me
I watched as the seconds turned to minutes
The minutes slowly made hours
The hours ticked away to days
The days painfully swapped places with weeks
The weeks exchanged titles with months
And the months changed with the seasons
Summer is now winter
And the house remains quiet

Help

Why is it?
Tears are about to fall
Nothing makes sense
Everything scares me
This coffee doesn't keep me awake
Won't someone help?
Please help me
The sun is shining bright
The house is dark as night
Don't answer the knock at the door
Please help
What is hope?
Hope is dead
I want to be given a fair chance
So much potential
So talented
I'm drowning in my fears
Help

Picture

I found your picture today...and laughed
There was nothing comical about the actual picture
I laughed because when I looked at it, I felt no
emotion
For the first time
I can look at you and feel nothing
I remember the day you gave me this picture
and in exchange I gave you my heart
I carried it everywhere
and showed it to whomever had eyes
I felt so much love each time I'd look at it
Then the dreaded day came when "we"
became just "me"
I'd look at this picture and
wonder how such a beautiful exterior
housed such an ugly person
Looking at this picture hurt
It reminded me of the
plethora of damage you inflicted
I hid this picture in attempt to
hide my pain
When I found it today
I laughed
No more love
No more hate
Nothing
It's just a picture

No Rhyme or Reason

A scream of pain...
... followed by silence
A collision with fate...
...followed by death
Questions without answers...
...followed by confusion
A heart full of love...
...followed by the remnants in pieces
Yesterdays laughter...
...followed by a lifetime of mourning
Too young to be taken away...
...followed by God's hidden agenda
Cries in the night...
...followed by another sleepless eve
Memories never forgotten...
...followed by a love that won't fade
A reunion of souls in the future...
...followed by tears of joy

By Writing This

By writing this I thought I could
revisit a place formally known as home
By writing this I thought I could
hold onto the drifting memory I never
wanted to lose
I can pretend I've moved on
and even lie to myself that I have
But no matter how many times
I tell myself this
I've learned my mind can't fool my heart
So by writing this I thought I could
trick my heart
into finally moving on
Looks like I thought wrong

4 Letter Necessity

Words screaming anger
...the reason unknown
Fists balled in fury
...clenched with confusion
A mind full of hate
...never a thought as to why
Laughs without smiles
...tears that don't fall
A body full of pain
...a soul tortured by truth
The most beautiful rainbow
...hidden by nature
A one word, four letter, necessity
... "H.E.L.P"

I Deeply Miss

Friday nights expecting nothing...
...but finding everything
Parties with beer in the glass...
...and the flavor of the week on tap
Summer PM's walking Main Street...
...until the tread on our shoes wore thin
Pre-game jitters...
...followed by that rush hearing my name announced
as a starter
That feeling when I'd score a goal...
...done up when I'd complete the hat trick
Conversations that started at sunset...
...and ended at sunrise
Three hour car rides...
...to get where we began
Not being in love...
...but the possibility

Nightmare

With each step forward the ancient ceiling lowers
The rancid sent of death steams out from the vents
Somewhere a little girl screams for help
As she screams its occurs that the red paint on the wall
isn't paint at all
A turn in the maze reveals its end
A giant black door hungrily awaits no more than 15
feet away
The already slow walk turns into an even more slothful
pace
Fear in the form of goose bumps overtakes every
ounce of flesh
A huge breath praying that it's not the last goes deep
in the lungs, as the black door stands only inches away
Dreadfully, the shaking hand pushes the door open...

The Ageless Question

He exits the coffin and re-enters the world
The scorching sun laughs onto his vitamin-malnourished
skin
A nervous twinge riffles down his legs as the cool
breeze wrestles with chimes
The ageless question echoes through his head
And the answer is punctuated as he retreats to his
coffin and slams the lid...

Discovery

The make it or break it test was issued and surprisingly
passed
The past 6 months have been a blessing in disguise,
also a necessity for survival
What have I done?
Not much to be honest
I read and I wrote poetry, helping open my eyes to a
new world, a world that has eagerly been   awaiting
me to discover it
I've made two essential friends
One, a Mr. Whitman, you can call him Walt
His writings have had a profound effect on my half
year and will forever on
Two, God
I guess I didn't just make friends with God because I've
known the guy my whole life, more or less
I just rediscovered him
And what I've learned...with God, anything is possible
and with poem nothing is impossible

Every Single Moment

Time is incomprehensible in its eternity
As time is indefinite, we are not
With each breath we take, "our time" draws closer to
completion
It's true that time is no man's friend
And it's also true we can't change what we've done
with our time
But what we can do...is "change"
We can change...here and now, to better our future
Make every single moment count
Live in the moment
Love
Love to the depths of our souls and tips of our toes
And add one word to our vocabulary and our
lives...the word "honesty"
Be honest, be brutally honest, be honest to a fault, just
be honest

Perfection

How do you describe perfection?
Don't be such a pessimist! It's there, I assure you
I like to think of perfection in the way there are those
hidden pictures hiding inside of a painting
You know the ones, the ones Yuppies had next to their
pool tables in the 90's
Some people can see the hidden picture right away,
while others will attempt standing on their   head to no
avail
The head-standers usually just need someone to point
out what's right in front of their noses
And just like those hidden pictures, once perfection is
seen, it can't be unseen!
But if you happen to be one that has trouble seeing
the inner painting, I'll point you down the right path
Here are a few places I found perfection
In the innocence of a child's laughter
Singing with the birds to a spring time sun rise
Watching the red, white, and blue, as our great
nation's flag grapples with the wind
That spark greater than love found only in your lovers
eyes
Trust me, if you look there, you'll finally see the
painting...and it will never go unnoticed again!!!

No Lifeguard on Duty

The four walls of hell continue ridiculing me
As the blizzard pours on another blanket of snow this
sunny July day
I walk more cautiously
You continue to remain a mystery that will never be
solved
I found that hidden ocean and am the first as foreseen
The rip tide flag is screaming to not swim
Have you ever been alone...and drowning?

Antenna

The aroma of ignorance burns my existence and fouls
the earth
Slowly the demise polluted river drains into the heavens
above
Twenty-seven days to prove your worth
Twenty-seven nights to realize you're never going to
succeed
Choices were made...hearts were broken
At times like these arrogance is a necessity
Yesterday's horse makes way for tomorrow's
anticipation
The continuous rapping from nowhere fills me with
comfort
I sympathize with the antenna waiting for lightning
That cave will keep you safe...but not forever
The world has proven you forever wrong...but you'll die
right
Open your eyes

Torn

No
Don't tell me you care
No
It's too late for that
Maybe
All the lies weren't at all
Maybe
What we had was real
Yes
I love you
Yes
I hate you
Maybe
I should give you another chance
Maybe
I should suck in my pride
No
There's a reason you're not here
No
Good-bye

My Secret

I need you like never before
Where can I find you
The same place as always I assume
Deep in the night
In those beautiful hours of never
You wait so patiently as I hurry to you
Your warm embrace welcomes and assures me that
you'll wait forever
You're my secret...and I'm yours
We needn't speak of love...that is a flower speaking of
water
But when the morning comes...you go
And, as the day's stresses bring me down, I smile
knowing there is always the night

The Itch

The itch grows with each breath
It's not what you think
You feel blood on your finger as you've unconsciously
scratched through the flesh on your left thigh
You look down confused as the skin around the nickel-
sized wound begins to bubble...almost as if it were
being burned from the inside
The itch intensifies
You watch in horror as a small black creature slowly
emerges from the wound
It's spider-like in appearance...but not at all
It scurries across your leg leaving a trail of blood in its
wake
In feared panic you try to smash the creature...but
your unsteady fist misses the mark
The creature is much too fast and you're much too
slow
Frantically it scurries back to the wound and painfully
squeezes back inside your body
The itch returns...this time with company, on the right
thigh also
You try with all your might to ignore them...but
eventually you scratch through flesh again...creating a
second hole to match the first
Both wounds begin to bubble
Sweat beads and falls off your forehead as you pray
for what's next to not occur
But it does...a creature from each hole angrily rips out
You scream in horror...temporarily causing both
creatures to retreat back inside you
The itch has you...it's just a matter of time

Confirmation

I sip the poison to stay alive
False hope lacerates into my being
The tree offers no support
How many ways must I document the facts?
The truth needn't lie
Failure is what you want
I refuse to oblige
The future holds my confirmation

Anniversary

It's been a year to the day since the break from reality
began
Coming back rings the alarm
Damaged relationships still hang in the balance
It was excused or so it was thought to be
The happy boy is gone
Don't bother looking...he isn't hiding this time
Never fear, the situation has improved...and continues
too
Don't wait
But never stop caring
Happy Anniversary

The Plan

The plan was simple...survive
Sometimes things don't go to plan
Maybe we just tried too hard
I was the fish and you were the aquarium
Engulfed in what you held
I saw you laugh as you fell and cracked open
The water poured effortlessly out of you
That hideous smile I now only see in nightmares
Love is just a word...and so is hate
The days go on
I believe the truth
Honestly

Buried

Everything comes into focus as the world goes blind
The answer lies buried too deep to ever locate
Touch your lips and you'll finally understand
The hand is red once again
I need it like you need air
I can't wake up
It's so hot...and keeps getting hotter
It went in easy
It came out painful
As long as you're alive...I'll be here

Uncertainty

This discussion always ends the same
The patronizing eyes stain my mind
When your dreams die...you don't have to with them
The rat continues his never-ending jog
Be strong...I know you can
The Ph.D... in uncertainty is blooming beautifully
There's a back way in to the door that was slammed
shut
We'll get there...be patient
Time has no meaning to forever
There's no place I could be than here with you
Give me a little credit
I refuse to watch you suffer
When you smile it's everything

You wait

In the room with little light you look at the clock
The numbers make no sense yet you stare in
admiration
You watch...
You watch as the seconds tick away the past and
climb to the future
You wait...
You forever wait for the light
A deep breath of dry humid air breezes under the door
You run your hand through your hair getting it tangled
in a mass of clumped sweat
You quietly ask the dark, "Who am I?"
You wait...
You forever wait for the light

It Begins

The grueling process begins
Picking and pulling
Adding and subtracting
Never knowing if it's good enough
Believing it is doesn't necessarily mean it is
Tomorrow will see the truth
It's time to test my work
No fears
Nothing but exceptional has been expressed
Then why am I nervous?

Forlorn

A role never seen...yet never going unheard
Sucking up the wretched
Abandoning the precious
The left shoulder won the war I never knew took place
Many close people became strangers
The unharmed were the forlorn...soon becoming my
allies
My eyes no longer served their initial purpose
Life became death and death became life
Salvation echoed within

Day to Forget

A session of time elapsed in constant disgust
The newly acquired pile of antique dirt will never
vanish
This day is so familiar
Please let me forget
I remember the last as it was my first
Tears were easier to come by than blood
The hunger has evaporated
Guns continue to rain hate in the night
When he spoke I should've listened
Ignorance is my only defense

Zombie

I've become a Zombie to my excess
Addicted to abnormality
Another harsh push towards the edge with each word
of conversation in the fake breeze
It's taking so much less as I crave so much more
Desire is beyond recollection
One more ounce of hate soils my mind
Feeling to not feel
That's no way to live

Annual

This was the day I brought you to your new home
I had a bed all cleaned and ready
When we arrived...I gave you a big drink and put you
in your bed
The next afternoon I smiled as you stood so tall in the
sunlight
The weeks passed and you were growing so big...so
fast
Some critics remarked that I was overfeeding you
but I disagreed
You looked perfectly healthy to me
The temperature began dropping and with it your
wholeness
With each day colder than the last...you struggled to
survive
Then just like that...you died
I brushed the snow off your green corpse
and whispered, "I'll see you next year."

Five Times

And so the tale goes
Five times
I've been in love f ve times
One, the instant I first saw you
Two, the instant you first smiled at me
Three, the instant I first smelled you
Four, the instant you first spoke to me
And five, the instant I first kissed you
Five times

Which Dimension

The door opens then slams shut
And opens once again
A man passes through
Which dimension this visit
"NO!" he screams with red eyes and sharp teeth
I shudder
Any portal but this would've been suffice
I look for safety in the dark of the night
Bright stars give away my net
"Run," a female voice whispers in my head
If only I could

When?

When you think of me...what do you think?
Do you think of the laughter?
Do you think of the tears?
What emotion do the tears produce?
Love? Anger? Guilt?
When you see me...what do you see?
Does it scare you?
Do you see me as I was or as I am?
When you talk to me...what do you hear?
The laughter of 1000 jokes or the suffering of 1000
weeps?
When will the questions end?
When?

Enraged Waterfall

I'll tell you what I can...what my memory allows
He pushed and I choked down two lung's full of terror
I drifted two feet in perfect harmony
Ever so slow the current pulled me out
Harmony quickly became horror
An overcompensation to the right resulted in a tip to
the left
My legs were stuck and submerged in the frigid water
My head went under
I tried screaming for help but got nothing out
The water rushed down my throat like an enraged
waterfall
And that's all I remember

The Way Home

It happened so fast
I was here then here no longer
When I opened my eyes the view had changed
In the same breath it remained exactly the same
I would do anything to not return
Anything!
I knew the unfortunate truth
Slowly I came back to before
To the place I'd die to not be
There's only one option
I need to find the way home

Wither

The scene was set
The timing was wrong
It was too late to retreat
Too little in front of me to have known
Is an undo out of the question?
Of course it is
The woods which were thought to be romantic were
anything but
Tears flushed out of your eyes
I ran in disappointment and you didn't follow
The footsteps were never revisited
I began to wither
There's not enough water and far too much time
The sun laughs sadistically

Rhyming Couplets and Free Rhyme

Gate 32

The snow was gently falling
on this December day
I looked to my right
and saw perfection's face
For her to be my girl
what I wouldn't pay
Long dark hair and big blue eyes
I wonder what's her name
My lips part but my brain freezes
I just want to say "hey"
Perfection is gone...but not forever
with a little help from fate

Fate

Perfection returned
this time on the phone
Somehow she got my number
my chance is not blown
Talking I'm nervous
just listen to my tone
Then I pull together
and get in the zone
Our first date's set
what should I wear
Does it really matter
with this funky hair
A shower and a shave
then I'll be prepared
As I ring her doorbell
I fill with fear
Perfection is so beautiful
no girl can compare
Her beauty makes my knees shake
quick I need a chair
She's so flawless
she is really great
We make plans for the next night
she said "don't be late"
She was everything I always dreamed
even after just one date
Perfection is my destiny
perfection is my fate

Insane

I'm driving in my car
off to the lake
Nobody is with me
I'm alone another day
Where is everyone?
it's getting so late

I stop at the intersection
look to my right
It's the little restaurant
where we had that huge fight
A smile fills my face
I try with all my might
But laughter fills the car
I feel high as a kite

The light turns green
I continue to drive
The laughter pours out
forcing tears from my eyes
If I drive off this cliff
no one would mind
The laughter won't stop
my throat begins to whine

Driving off the cliff
doesn't seem so lame
And the result would leave
no more depression and no more pain
This drink isn't helping
it's messing with my brain
The only explanation
is I'm going insane

I Awake

I awake from reality
and begin to dream
This makes no sense
when I only live to sleep
It wasn't always this bad
once life had meaning
Every single day now
follows the same routine
I awake all alone
then begin to dream

The day you left
was the day I died
You showed no remorse
when I began to cry
How the hell could you do this?
please tell me why
I thought we were perfect
yet another lie
I hate myself for this
but I'd give it one more try

The best and the worst thing
all rolled into one
I guess stomping on my emotions
to you is pretty fun
The hardest part for me
is admitting we are done

When I sleep and when I wake
I don't feel the same
In my dreams I'm with you
for that I feel ashamed
In the night that spark we shared
is still a burning flame
Morning comes and you're not there
my body fills with pain

Is It Real

You say you're in love
it's just something you feel
Which begs the question
can it be real?
"Of course" I'd once answer
for I had a great deal
Then it was gone
and my heart began to peel

Now I question
the sanctity of love
Even the sweetest of girls
I no longer can trust
The dagger left in me
is quickly growing rust

The days are so quiet
even the birds don't sing
Being betrayed by her
was the worst kind of sting
I wonder if it was worth it
her little fling
In the blink of an eye
she demolished our dream

Forgive me when I see her next
if I begin to scream
At least with her help
I learned one little thing
Love isn't real
it's for the naive

Return

I unlocked the door
and entered my home
A quick look around
sent chills to my bones
My belonging were gone
my valuables taken
I started to tremble
my knees began shaking
It didn't take long
to discover the guilty party
The drug addict devil
time for me to rally
You stole what I had
so you could get high
I hoped in my car
time for a drive
I gave you what I could
but you needed more
Just wait till I find you
you thieving little whore
First stop your parents
lucky you weren't there
I'm sure mom and dad
wouldn't like you with bloody hair

Next stop your friend's
your car not at his place
Too bad for him
he could've seen me break your face
I need to pull it together
I need to calm down
I need to find that bitch
and beat her to the ground
I slam on the brakes
and look into my brain
Why stoop to her level
a cunt who is insane
I burn all your pictures
and kiss you goodbye
It's truly fucked up
how you live to get high
I wonder what will happen
only time will tell
At this rate you'll soon be dead
and return to hell

Aubrey

It returned to my heart
that feeling of lust
The love for another
the ability to trust

In the wink of an eye
bad switched to good
Depression disappeared
just like it should

Your beautiful smile
your long dark hair
Am I only dreaming?
Can this be real?

Not a second since we met
have you not stole my thoughts
A woman so beautiful
A woman so smart

Last time I fell
I mistook horns for wings
But that winter is over
I'm ready for spring

That day in the park
out under the tree
My soul was returned
I thank you Aubrey

Joy

We all have a hero
one we wish we could be
Mine is my sister
she's a hero to me

When she's scared
she doesn't run and hide
She stands up for what she believes
showing nothing but pride

We share the same genes
and suffer the same fate
Where she learned to love
I learned to hate

Her courage is uncanny
her fight is unreal
I want to be like her
I want to again feel

She has managed to turn
bad into good
I'm trying to be like her
I know that I could

My hero is my sister
she is the real McCoy
I love her to death
my hero named Joy

Rum

Another day off the calendar
down the shoot another drink
Just like the titanic
eventually he will sink
Help he rejects
refusing to just think
His liver begs for a break
and forgot the color pink

He can fix all my problems
when we speak on the phone
But he won't put the glass down
and try to fix his own
It's getting horribly bad
his muscle barely clings to bone
His skin is turning yellow
he never leaves home

Once he mumbled
"drinking is what I do, I don't want to stop"
What am I to do?
after all he is my pop
I can't force him not to
I can't call the cops
This is a dilemma
I don't want him to drop

The grim reaper is on the way
slowly here he comes
Nothing will stop his arrival
not even the most powerful gun
I wait and I watch
this is anything but fun
He will die with his best friend
a big glass of rum

Independence

The scent of hot dogs and hamburgers
filled the air
Families gathered in backyards across the nation
without a care
Everyone was in good spirits
I felt nothing but fear
Something was wrong
my heart began to tear
I soon realized
no fireworks for me this year

The sun was scorching hot
my skin was bitter cold
What's eating at my inside
I need the truth be told
The angel is standing in an alley
pointing down a depressing road
I may only be 22
but today I feel very old

Hours before the colorful expositions
I fall fast asleep
I'm too upset to go out
too confused to eat
I know perfection is gone
she made a copy of the key
Her heart was expensive
for others it was free

A fitting day to do this
a bad day to cry
Your family is so supportive
still I don't know why
I lay in bed and dream of you
I would rather die
On this nation's day of independence
what of shit filled 4th of July

Cry

Ornaments filled the tree
with lights shining green, red, and blue
It's been some time
but my thoughts fell on you

A day of joy...a day of light
A day of fear...a day of fright

Tons of beautifully wrapped presents
were stacked under the tree
The little ones were filled with turkey
and also filled with glee

Santa was making his rounds
and soon to be on his way
Rudolf with his red nose
another year in the lead of the sleigh

The family was gathered
and all in place
The obviously fake smile
filled my face

Some days are good
some days are bad
Some days are happy
this day was sad

Perhaps because
it was our first Christmas apart
Whatever it was
you were there in my heart

While others celebrated
the birth of Christ
I felt the wound get deeper
my soul turned cold as ice

When I got home...I looked to the sky
no Santa in sight
I began to cry

Devil

Is she an angel or a devil?
it's impossible to tell
Don't be lured in
by her intoxicating smell

She fell from heaven
and landed on her feet
Down from above
put her for me

Or...did she come from below
and land on her knees
Read the fine print
"next in line take a seat"

Beauty and brains
as bad a combo as it is good
When addiction is added to the equation
run is what you should

No angel would ever think
of doing what you've done
Thank my lucky stars you're gone
in that way I won

So when you notice your angel
sprout some horns
Send her back to hell
where she was REALLY spawned

Best Friend

One definite thing
is time surely flies
It seems like minutes ago
we met in junior high

I thought I was so cool
in my purple Jordan's and green Skidz
Your passion was hockey and girls
we were 12 year old kids

Our friendship began
in Mr. Norman's history class
I snapped the girl in front of my desk's bra
while you let me copy so I'd pass

In band we both played the sax
me the alto and you the baritone
Mr. Bishop was my favorite teacher
that podium was his throne

The first time we hung out
we played video games till we were sick
That was the day I swore your mom
would someday be my chick

High school was different
things went up and down
You were the heart throb
and I was the class clown

Our group of friends
were all right on the whole
Most were real morons
with the intellect of trolls

Things have really changed
since we were those goofy kids in junior high
Now you're a cop
with Debi by your side

But one thing remains
and will to the very end
We'll always be there for one another
you are my best friend

Reflection

I look in the mirror
but that's not my face
The reflection shows a scared little boy
not a man of my age

The longer I look
the more fear I see
Why am I so spooked
what can it be

I watch a bead of sweat
slowly trickle down my head
The look in my eyes
expresses nothing but dread

I don't recognize the reflection
even though I know it's me
My body begins to shiver
that's a sight I pray never again to see

Fantasy

Her beauty radiates onto me
her words flow so sweet
She embodies perfection
we've yet to meet

I've seen her more than once
but only when I sleep
The object of my affection
is but a fantasy

Her skin is so soft
it feels smooth as silk
A smile that draws me in
lips I want to kiss

The middle of her back
is where her gorgeous hair rests
One stare into her beautiful brown eyes
and I can feel my heart bounce crazily in my chest

Tight little jeans
and a bright blue shirt
Being with her
I know I'd end up hurt

I see no flaws
she is perfect as can be
her name is Liz
she is my fantasy

Fake

Shut your eyes and think real hard
what one word do you find
When I think of you I'm full of anger
the word "fake" fills my mind

On the friendship scale from one to ten
I give you a negative three
Maybe you should hang out with a dog
and learn the meaning of loyalty

Everyone knows you're pathetic
everyone but you
You think you're so special
you think you're so cool

My only solace is knowing
one day you'll see the truth
That you burned too many bridges
in the process destroyed your youth

You told so many lies
they became your reality
You must of got it from your mom
her and her false hospitality

Whenever you screwed up
I took the blame
Now I wish I hadn't
so you could of felt the shame

You've departed town en route
to the land of musical ignorance
I couldn't be happier
no more of you and your fake appearances

Because of you

Because of you
I am what I am
You helped me be a boy
and are guiding me down a the path to be a man

Looking back I realize
what an amazing job you've done
Raising two children
all on your own

Through thick and thin, good and bad
you've always been there for me
I know I haven't been the best son
someday...I will be

When life went and got in the way
of my goals and my dreams
You kept my hope alive and
I could always count on you to be on my team

I honestly can say
you've been the most special person to me
You're the best mother a kid could have
I'm sure Joy would agree

You deserve the best
and I'm so glad you've found Tom
And for all the times it went unsaid
don't forget, I love you mom

Feet

Somethings are so repulsive
that when seen you want to retreat
Everyone has two of these
ugly, smelly feet

They come
in all different sizes and shapes
No matter how big or small
when exposed I look for the quickest escape

Some come equipped with fungi infected nails
others have long and skinny toes
No matter what they produce
when in view it's chunks I want to blow

Whoever said the human body is a beautiful thing
must of meant from the ankles up
But if he did mean the whole body
feet included, he is a real chump

Sweaty, pale, hairy, stinky
curly toed, bacteria infected feet
Please keep them covered
especially after a day in the heat

Feet are disgusting
and feet are gross
Feet are unworthy
of this little poem

Fleece

My heart was chopped up
piece by piece
But then there you were
in that bright red fleece

One by one
you helped piece the puzzle back to whole
You first cleansed my heart
and then cleansed my soul

I never thought
I could once again smile so bright
You showed me how disquietingly wrong she was
and showed me how I was right

I guess what I'm trying to say
is I'll be forever in debt to you
You showed me there's life to be lived
I've never said anything more true

Relapse

My mouth opens
and the anger pours out
I try to calm down
I can't help but shout

You took your life
and this situation for granted
You're a great magician
you really had me enchanted

You play with emotions
like they're a game
You're so messed up
you think you're destined for fame

It's horribly sad
your life has become a joke
Whenever you get down
you run for the coke

I tried with all my might
to help you and your life
I wanted nothing more
than you as my wife

But now I realize
between us falls too many gaps
And my heart can't take
the inevitable relapse

Promise

Those notes you wrote me
I've kept them all
When I read them at night
I don't feel so small

To say you're missed
is the understatement of this lifetime
The mountain of my world
now seems impossible to climb

I miss your gentle touch
I miss your soft lips
I miss your sense of humor
I miss your sexy hips

How do you move on
when you've tasted perfection
I don't want to call anyone else
the object of my affection

One day I'm going to wake up
from this living nightmare
And your spot on the bed
won't be occupied by air

I made a promise
and I intend to hold true
We'll be together again
my heart is not through

Beast

Hairy, smelly, funny
fat little beast
How did I get so lucky
you're the sweetest thing

Fetch, walks
and tug o war
Taking care of you
is my favorite chore

You're happy to see me
anytime of the day
Especially at night
when its time to play

"Crazy baby runs"
and stuffed animals in shreds
You're pure comedy
with that undersized head

You think you're a lap dog
even though you weigh a ton
The days it's snowy out
is when you have the most fun

Together we terrorize
the orange little cat
Now he always hides
because he is a brat

When you snore at night
it's the cutest thing
I love you so much
my chubby little beast

Steinquist

Sixteen and nervous
empty as can be
Hormones out of whack
does she like me

My first real crush
I don't know how to act
Her lips are so luscious
that's a matter of fact

Hanging out with her
my head fills with secret fantasies
If she knew the truth
I guarantee she'd flee

Now I understand
why they call it a crush
Because the feelings are one-sided
and hurt very much

Maybe one day
she'll feel the same as me
That's pretty doubtful
I'm just nervous and sixteen

Curse

Life is a long, hard,
scary journey
Especially when the only sure thing
is one day being covered up on a gurney

For some, the American dream
gets dragged through the slush
As bad as they may want it
life dealt them a pair of deuces instead of a royal flush

"They" say when handed lemons
make lemonade
I say if "they" walked a step in my shoes
their little saying would change

"When life throws you a curve ball
just adjust your stance"
Whoever is coming up with this bullshit
must be in a trance

Not everyone is given
a life worth living
It's not our fault
but God remains unforgiving

There's not a damn thing I can do
but watch it grow worse
There is no happy ending to this story
my life is but a curse

Come Back

I think I've waited
a tad too long
You were always right
and I was always wrong

I watch the phone
as it remains quiet
My soul needs to hear your sweetness
or it threatens to riot

You left a note
when time expired
History remembers that
as the day my heart retired

My two new friends
go by the names, Pain and Suffering
I still smell your beauty
and still hear you sing

Whenever you would knock
I would let you in
I wish I always hadn't worn
such a sinister grin

Meet me in the future
and try to forget the past
We really need to hurry
this life is going fast

Oneself

Ask yourself this:
do you know who you are?
I'm not talking about your age,
sex, job, or even about your car

I'm asking about the inside
the person no one else knows
The person who hates music
but is screaming to compose

That's just an example
of what could be waiting for you to find
I think you'll be amazed
if you give it some time

Everyone is different
but most act the same
Never taking the time to discover oneself
truly is a shame

So the next time you find
a few extra minutes alone
Introduce yourself to your inside
I'm anxious to see what grows

Sunday

When we made our plans to spend eternity together
we forgot one thing
We forgot that early summer Sunday
filled with sorrow and filed with pain

The words we exchanged
that humid sweaty night
Would be the 12th round
in this equally fought fight

You summed up your anger
with a slap in my face
That horrible final memory
is impossible to erase

All the great times we shared
are good as forgotten
All that remains now
is this feeling that is rotten

My only hope is you remember
some good and not all bad
Because at times we were perfect
at times we weren't sad

Crow

It's not the cold that keeps me inside
it's my emotions
Everything seems to be progressing
in extremely rapid motion

The never-ending hurt
is my one true companion
The never-ending emptiness matches
the depth in the grand canyon

This pain will not cease
running from head to toe
My eyes are peeled open
in search for the crow

This will only result in
the termination of my life
Sometimes I think it'd be better
to go and find a knife

But I wait and I watch
I pray and I cry
No matter what happens
soon I will die

Nirvana

There is a place
that no one else knows
There is a place
when scared I like to go

The waves welcome me
with their usual crash
Nothing is wrong here
worries dissipate in a flash

The sun brings the heat
no matter what time of year
The one and only rule is
to have no more fear

My friends here
are the fish and this iguana
Everyone should have
their own personal nirvana

Perfect Day

Have you ever had a day
when everything goes right
From the second the alarm clock wakes you
until the final kiss goodnight

It starts off simple
with the perfect hair
When you leave home
you don't forget a prayer

You find a note in your pocket
which reads "I love you"
A smile takes over your face
as your feelings for that special someone just grew

Every question asked
you have a witty reply
The boring hours of the day
just seem to cruise by

Your boss asks you into his office
for a minute of your day
You think you're getting fired
but instead you get a raise

When you get home
your lover is waiting with open arms
You don't even try
but out flows your charm

The dinner is fabulous
and the movie is too
You whisper to God
goodnight and thank you

Dumped

I just stopped by
to see how you're doing
You answer the door with tears
and we get the coffee brewing

I know how you're feeling and
my heart hurts to see you going through this
It's such a hard emotional battle
when a week ago you were filled with bliss

We laugh and we talk
ignoring the issue
Knowing if it's brought up
you'll need more tissues

He doesn't deserve
a woman as special as you
Just give it some time
and you won't feel so blue

I kiss your pretty hair
as I turn to leave
You'll find love again
you just need to believe

Hug Police

Quick there she goes
I need to apprehend her
before my chance is blown

She is a fugitive
and I'm the hug police
The longer I wait
the more my opportunity will decrease

I carry no night stick
and I've got no guns
I use my two arms
and give those in need hugs

I know no hate
I only know love
Please make this easy
I don't like to shove

"inspired by my beast"

Oliver

I take care of you
like you were my own
You refuse to listen
when I scream at you "NO"

I feed you when you're hungry
and bathe you when you stink
The way you don't acknowledge my presence
is driving me to the brink

All you seem to care about
is killing mice and climbing trees
I know you miss the litter box on purpose
when it's time for you to pee

As soon as the light goes off
you jump around on the bed
I cringe at the thought
of the sleepless nights ahead

You are orange
and you are bad
You better straighten out mister
I'm starting to get mad

Tom

We never had
what's defined as "the good life"
It's not fair to her
she is such a great mom and would be an equally
great wife

It was just the three of us
two kids and our mom
Then came a savior
going by the name of Tom

He showed her
that being sad wasn't her fate
I'm so happy seeing her
all dressed up for a date

He taught me
a bunch of things I never knew
Simple things like respect and honesty
and if something breaks just apply a little glue

He gave all of us a life
and all of us a home
I thought I would thank him
with this little poem

Ecstasy

You lived to be carried away
by overwhelming emotion
Even if the only means of getting there
were various death potions

It was understood a relationship
with you would be artificial
However you had more than one thing
that I found beneficial

We took and we gave
to match the others needs
This situation had planted
many awful seeds

Your skin was too white
and your eyes were constantly dilated
It's truly hard to fathom
together what we'd created

There's no way out
nor a way to change the past
Tomorrow is your funeral
I hope you had a blast

Insomnia

My brain cries for sleep
my eyes try to close
The minutes go so fast
the hours go so slow

One of life's necessities
seems to have escaped me
I look with all my might
but I can't find sleep

The night becomes the day
and the day becomes the night
The sun is so dull
where the moon is so bright

I'd give everything I posses
for an evening of peace
These demons in my head
simply refuse to cease

Another sleepless night
is about to go in the books
Looks like Insomnia tricked the Sandman
what a lousy filthy crook

Off to College

Tomorrow is the day
you go away to college
Supposedly to help increase
your intellect and knowledge

This'll be the first obstacle
in our relationship
Everyone keeps whispering long distance
is a bumpy trip

We've made it this far
we can beat anything
Don't forget our pact
and I want you to have my class ring

We'll talk every night
and visit on the holidays
We can make this work
because our love is real...not a game

Black

Just another night
of this pointless existence
Drunk beyond belief
with the walls as my assistants

The baby gets aborted
without a second thought
A life is terminated
for our own faults

The screams do their job
and silence the pain
With any luck this memory
will wash away with the rain

Trying to not drown
in the sea of depression
The rip tide won't halt
with its awful aggression

The smile is always there
and the answer is always "yes"
The life blood has turned black
it started in the chest

Hurt

I never meant to hurt you
but I did
You let feelings enter this
that's what blew the lid

What we had was perfect
but you wanted more
Unfortunately I didn't
which started your heart to pour

Now when I call
you just let it ring
We should of stopped this
when you began to cling

Your heart was broke
and so was our friendship
Like sand through my fingers
we began to sift

You were a great friend and
I will always care about you
for all the lies I told
that is the one truth

Almost there

The future has the answer
the past asks the question
Everyday is a little scarier
turning into an unhealthy obsession

Silence is not the way
communication is a must
Friends make better enemies
no one's left to trust

Face to face
with all my fears
Death is so far away
yet life is still not here

Monday is the same as Friday
and morning is the same as night
Just a little more time
and everything will be all right

Roller Coaster

She's a roller coaster
never finding a straight stretch of track
At any seeming second
her sanity will crack

When she is slowly clanking skyward
up to the top
She's queen of the world
nothing can make her stop

Then comes the downward free-fall
at unimaginable speeds
It's here and now her mission's to hurt and kill
and wow does she succeed

She's a different person
from one day to the next
Impossible to figure out
defining the word complex

She needs to seek help
before it is too late
Next stop the ultimatum to change
or never again see me walk through her amusement
park gate

Gray

The hallway is so silent
your absence is so loud
The floor is scuffed up
there's no lining on this cloud

The balance beam has shattered
the pendulum is swaying
To the right is sanity
to the left the monster begins preying

The traffic remains backed up
leaving out of the question
My ears continue bleeding
from your appalling confession

Everything is painted black
nothing left is white
This situation is grim
becoming a woeful plight

The calendar consists of
three hundred and sixty five days
Maybe this year one
won't be stained in gray

Go

The lack of challenge
is what drives me away
Almost as if no matter what I do
I've already won this game

I don't want
what's there for the taking
That's too easy
without the excitement of breaking

Why is it the harder
I push you to go
The more intense and deeper
your feelings grow?

I'm not understanding how
to end a situation like this
My only option left seems
whenever I see you…look for the nearest exit

Waiting

I've been
waiting for a good day
The only color
I see is gray
My body slowly
begins to decay
The law of gravity
is hard to obey
The game of life
is getting so hard to play
My life is full of regret
including today
Everything out here
is so cliché
Not one has been answered
yet I continue to pray
Will this ever
go away
Or somehow
start to delay
There will be
no need for a replay
Still waiting
for a good day

Karma

I see it time
and time again
There must be a short
in every mans brain

Men cheat on, lie to, and disrespect their women
in every possible way
But they never once fathom
their lover would stray

For that men are vulnerable
and for that men are weak
For that women are sly
and for that women are sleek

When Karma comes around
to bite men in the ass
They don't know how to take it
feeling that day is their last

If men would treat women
like the queens they are
Their relationship would be more
than just a painful scar

Apparently that's the way
the world today works
Men continue to self-destruct
because we are jerks

Twister

We've tried to figure out
how this can be
It's impossible
is all we can agree

Your words wrap around me
like a June twister
My heart feels as if its exploding
like a puss-filled blister

Just be patient
this is so new to me
But don't worry
you're the only one with a key

I'll let you in
the instant I'm ready
Try to not rock the boat
keep it nice and steady

I hope when I finally get there
it's not too late
It'd be unfair
to make you promise to wait

I see you in the distance
I'm almost there
Slow down a little
what we have is so rare

Running Thin

The days are getting old
and beginning to run thin
The earth remains unaffected
and continues it's spin

Life can be such a dirty game
at the same time an amazing gift
The joke with no punch line begins
when one begins to drift

The return to the familiar darkness
forever will remain a mixture of emotion
My hope is that the beauty
can somehow compare to the Caribbean Ocean

To all my family
I love you, health and no harm
When it's your time to go to heaven
I'll greet you with open arms

Again

Your timing is impeccable
here you are once again
Of course I question your motives
what have you to gain

I'm as foolish as a jester
and excited as a summer day
I'll put my heart out there
and wait for the inevitable slay

Together we make magic
apart I turn to stone
Deep down I felt your return
somehow I'd already known

I look at the calendar
you've been gone an eternity as of last week
Hearing your voice again
I lose the ability to speak

I hope this time
you don't pull my heart out like before
Besides I do believe it's my turn
to even up the score

Rapture

Her head begins pounding
so she pops a pill
Ignoring the danger
ignoring the chill

In no time flat
she feels good as new
Even the most complex problem
becomes easy to construe

Hours fly by
in this constant rapture
Sobriety on her heels
but unable to capture

The walls come to life
the words float away
Her defenses have been stiffened
keeping the demons at bay

The spiral begins twirling
and down she slowly sinks
Her head hurts again
she's unable to think

So she pops a pill...

Better Days

I'll never give in
I'll continue to fight
Tomorrow will be better
black will turn to light

Something deep inside
is screaming to survive
Happy days are fast approaching
I can't wait to arrive

This is the day
when things started to change
I traded tears for smiles
in the first of many exchanges

Ocean

When I talk to you
a feeling fills my heart
A feeling poetry can't capture
a feeling more beautiful than art

I ache for your words
and scream for your touch
It baffles me to think
that I like you this much

I lay awake at night
imagining you next to me
That feel of your hair against my chest
fills me with glee

Six months and an ocean
now separates me to you
Is that too much of an obstacle?
if only I knew

Dreamer

What do we have
if we don't have dreams
We don't have much
that's how it seems

If you're reading this poem
my dream has been found
My advice is never give up
as corny as that sounds

Never half-ass it
give it your all
Chances are before you fly
you're going to have to fall

Lock on to what you want
and never lose your sight
Be prepared for a little pain
this won't be an easy fight

You can do whatever
it is you want to in your life
Be it a doctor, a lawyer,
an actor or even find the perfect wife

Wonder

It made me wonder when she asked:
When was the last time your smile was real?
How long has it been since your soul could feel?
Did you ever consider talking with Satan about a deal?
What's the point of all the praying, honestly what's the appeal?
What did God ever do besides give you a normal life then crush it under his heel?
When she asked, it made me wonder:

Happiness

I'm happiest in life when I have
a blank piece of paper and an open mind
I start jotting down idea's
amazed at what I find

Emotions flow from my pen
like water from a tap
Feelings that are jumbled inside
but when written become clear as a map

Things never seem as bad
when I'm writing how I feel
I can teleport to a different life
a life I wish was real

I'm glad I found something
I've got such a passion to do
To each his own they say
what is happiness to you?

24 Hours

Believe it when told
"what a difference a day can make"
For instance 24 hours ago
I felt I was going to break

Some days the thought of tomorrow
may not always seem better
Just remember, no matter how cold the chill
you can always put on a sweater

At the time, everything seems worse
than it truly is
Take a step back from the situation
before you fail this quiz

Being a bitter, mad person
is a waste of your time
To feel happy can be achieved
without committing a crime

Just decide to be happy
it's not a hard choice
Put on a genuine smile
to help silence depression's voice

So next time you think
your life is too hard to take
Stop and think what a difference
24 hours can make

K.D.H

In a life full of regrets
one stands out the most
I was too young to realize how special you were
and since no one's come close

I smile every time
you find your way into my mind
I can't believe I blew my chance
I truly must of been blind

You were my first taste of happiness
and my first sip of love
You showed me the meaning of life
and what I'm capable of

We didn't need anything but each other
to be truly happy
I find it comical how the very thought of you
makes me so sappy

The point to this poem
is to not seem bitter and blue
I just wanted to let you know what you meant
and to tell you...thank you

Pawn

It really makes me wonder
why it wasn't me, but you
Your tainted memory enters my soul
then passes right through

Long days forgotten
the happiness is gone
I'll never understand how
you played me like a pawn

The bitter taste of euphoria
is all that remains
That sour memory of you
is coated with nothing but pain

With every single raindrop
I still see your face
Finally with the vision I feel no more love
not even a trace

No Other Way

I just want to sleep
but you won't go away
You dance in my head
like children at play

I turn on a light
and head to my desk
Oh what you do
you cause nothing but stress

If I don't write you down
you won't let me sleep
You're worse than my alarm clock
with that ear-wrenching beep

Out of my mind
I smile so bright
I head back to bed
off goes the light

Sleep is so near
I begin to dream
Then there you are
with a piercing loud scream

I grab my pen
what a long day
I'd honestly went it
no other way

Manic

You're happy
You're sad
You're delighted
You're mad

You love
You hate
It's horrid
It's great

You're up
You're down
It's blue
It's brown

You walk
You run
It's boring
It's fun

Do us all a favor
and make up your mind
So today are you mean
or today are you kind?

Awry

Can I ask you a question
and please don't respond with a lie
Is there anything you fear more
than the horrifying day when you die
I've laid awake many nights
trying to make sense of the universal question "why"
But the only thing I conclude is confusion
followed by fear and the occasional cry
I wonder with not one shed of proof
if there really is a God in the sky
Or if religion is some fictional story
created to help cope with mortality by some
frightened little guy
I haven't sold any stock in God yet
but I refuse to tell my broker to buy
All I'm saying is if religion was an ocean
to me it'd almost be dry
My faith is still present
don't get me wrong I'll never deny
I guess it's just one of those days
when everything seems awry

Change

It's hard to ask for
what you want or need
But without some help
that wound continues to bleed

Take my advice
don't wait until it's too late
The road that may seem full of turns
with help...could actually be very straight

So whatever it is
your soul requires...speak up
That empty glass of soda
may easily become an overfilled cup

The beauty of change
is it can happen in the wink of an eye
And when whatever is holding you down is gone
you'll feel like you can fly

Noose

Ignorance is bliss
knowledge equals concern
The enormous lifeless ocean
slowly begins to burn

The mirror crashes down
into a mass of shattered hope
The set of shaking hands
completes a noose in the rope

The time ticks to now
and the hour rings grim
Soon the heart will match
the inanimate limbs

There is no yield
to the inevitable truth
Perhaps this is a prime example
of another wasted youth

The Bait

Screams yelling anger
from the attic full of hate
You remain content
playing the role as my bait

You ask me with laughter
"do you want to die"
Startled, I answer "no"
then the curious question..."why"

You begin to shake
I whisper, "I didn't mean to scare you"
You demand of me an answer
and I'd give one if I knew

As the full moon glows down
an eerie shade of green
The dirt-coated house
remains immaculately clean

The flagitious plot is unfolding
exactly to my plan
A sinister smile realizes...this'll soon be over
before it even began

Storm

The fire refuses to extinguish
as does my disgust
The only common ground
is this undeniable lust

When the clock chimes ten
be ready to run
I recommend not stopping
until we see the sun

It feels so good
to breathe fresh air
Could this finally be our answer
to all of these prayers

Lightning never comes
without it's ally thunder
With every storm's end
I remain full of wonder

Story of my Life

The sleep full of optimism
The dreams full of lies
The night full of laughter
The morning full of cries
The novel with no ending
The car that won't drive
The flower that won't bloom
The bird that won't fly
The feet that won't run
The departure without goodbye
The hand that won't play
The story of my life

You

Who are you
I'd like to know
Could you be the girl
I knew years ago

You're so beautiful
in the most repulsive way
The amount I love you is overshadowed
by the immense amount of hate

You build me up
just to let me down
For every smile you throw my way
consequently come two frowns

Remember when we used to kiss
and it'd seem sparks would fly
Now when I get near your lips
snow falls from the sky

I miss the heart
that used to take resident under your skin
I've looked for it to no avail
where has it been?

Once Again

The deception once again
fooled the naive
Once again it dies
and once again she leaves

Looking back I miss
everything that was
Especially the intense feeling we call
the honeymoon phase buzz

I keep getting lost
in the nothingness inside
For all the pain I feel
you continue your lies

I drink down my glass of pathetic
with a splash of desperation
In my never-ending hour of pain
somewhere I know is your sixty minute celebration

Once again you win
and once again I lose
Once again you'll come back
maybe this time I'll refuse

Hate

I hate the mumbles
that I consider talk
I hate the stumbles
that I consider walk

I hate that I have no memory
of laughter or fun
I hate this sad, depressed
soul that I've become

I hate that even on sunny days
all I see is rain
I hate with each step
my joints scream with pain

I hate the thought
of my diminishing health
What I hate most
I hate myself

Divorce

If I know what I knew
my reality wouldn't be real
Fictional stories by both
in attempt to increase their appeal

The odds continue to remain
never in my favor
The love you both showered me in
I'll forever savor

It always has to come down
to one or the other
No kid should have to choose
between his father or his mother

Unfortunately that's how it goes
and will to the end of time
The parent chosen feels like king
while the other feels like slime

The truth is no one wins
in a situation like this
Neither of the parents
and especially not the kid

Summer of 97

Everyone remembers a time
that they often compare to heaven
For some it may be a moment, others perhaps a day,
for me it was the summer of 97

Now this was a time
when everything made sense
This was my calm before the storm
before everything got so damn intense

It started off beautifully
graduating one of the top in my class
The beauty wasn't in graduating
it was knowing that highschool was in the past

The parties began
the very next day
I don't think they stopped
until the following May

Me and a few friends
made a habit of going to concerts
Because of the hard hill at Pine Knob
my ass still hurts

The Red Wings won their first cup
in something like 42 years
The H-crowd cruised the five nine
to participate in the cheers

I can't put into words
the pure bliss of the summer of 97
The one and only thing I don't miss
is having a curfew of eleven

Woodstone

We moved in
and started a new life
Me minus a mother and a sister
you minus a daughter and a wife

The adventure known as Woodstone
is coming to an end
In the past 7 years
it's made quite a few friends

What a crazy ride
Woodstone has given
For all the pain inflicted
I know we are forgiven

It's here life was discovered
and here life was lost
Beautiful spring days followed
by the summer covered in frost

The departure will be best described
as one that's bittersweet
The best and worst years of my life were spent here
I'll leave feeling complete

"Great"

Do you honestly think
I don't know what you did
Every time you speak to me
I've an urge to rip off your head

What a "great" friend
you've proven to be
My hate started off small
but has bloomed into a fully-grown tree

Out of all my friends
from you I expected more
No offense but I don't think your intelligence
matches that IQ score

My disgust grows
with every look into your eyes
And when I look hard
I see the former bond as it slowly begins to die

I just wanted
to let you know that I know
And tell you between us things will never again be
good
...like they were years ago

Is This Hell?

I really don't think
this is what God had in mind
A world full of hate, disease, terror,
to be blunt a world of crime

I like to think God has been on vacation
for the past couple hundred years
Because what I don't like is the thought of Him
knowing of all the sickness, hunger, killing and despair

You're born and then you die
the in-between is al we have
A life undoubtedly full of sadness and tragedy
a world that makes me screaming mad

Is this hell?
this world where danger is always brewing
This world where the starving remain hungry and the ill
remain sick
this has to be the Devil's doing...right?!

One-Man Army

The one-man army
continues his fight
It begins when he wakes
till deep into the night

His body is worn down
and covered in pain
This never-ending resolution
is driving him insane

With each battle won
another is lost
He wonders if his life
is worth this war's cost

Land of Laughs

If I pretend it's not there
maybe it'll go away
If it only worked like that
all would be okay

In this land of fiction
I'll tell ya how it'd be
I would be the scientist
with a cure for every disease

There'd be no room for depression
nor a reason to cry
Only room for happiness
in this land of laughs and smiles

I'll hold onto this place
as long as I can
Because without it's comfort
I'm just a scared little man

Bird

I wish I was a bird
I'd fly away to a place foreign and strange
I'd fly to a land where I'm accepted
without having to change

I'd not be the ideal "bird"
in this day and age
As a result, "they'd" keep
me locked in their cage

When will someone let me free
so I can spread my wings
Because this bird has many beautiful colors
and numerous songs to sing

The Key

No one's ever tried
to weather the storm
They must not understand after the blizzard
comes days that are warm

Maybe warm
isn't good enough heat
Perhaps you need July Kentucky sun
and just lie when we meet

Life has a way of kicking you square in the balls
when everything finally seems right
There will always tomorrow
but I miss you tonight

There's no company
but the streetlights and the rain
I wish I had the key
to unlock my heart from this chain

Words

You can't take back
the words that you've said
So make sure to think
before the world knows what's in your head

Cause once it's out...it's out
and there's no going back
Everyone is different
a compliment to her...to him is an attack

Never be ashamed of who you are
or what you think
But be mindful of your words
because some can make you sink

The Ghastly Road

I want my innocence
I want to be pure
I want laughter
I want a cure

So many things
I've taken for granted
Life's been so deviant
since the demon seed's been planted

The permanent January
drips another bead of blood
I stand at the gates
anticipating the flood

Many times I've peeped
down the ghastly road
Wondering how many more beats
until the firecracker explodes

I want my innocence
I want to be pure
I want laughter
I want a cure

Sleep Strike

Seventy three hours
and going strong
Unfortunately this sleep strike
is one hundred percent wrong

Why does this happen
time and time again
My body refuses to fall asleep
yet every ounce screams in pain

The circles under my eyes
are maturing with the time
Blocking any chance of seeing
dreams that are divine

I need to install an on/off switch
somewhere in my head
But who would turn it back on?
please let me go to bed!

5:29a.m.

Is

The season is the mood
the song is the bird
The voice is so soft
forever going unheard

The fear is tomorrow
the tear is today
The timing that was perfect
was also very late

The pain is the truth
the love is the lie
It really was never worth
giving the old college try

The smoke is the alarm
the white-coat is the hope
The ever changing status
makes it impossible to cope

The scream is the silence
the tale is never told
The blanket won't warm
the soul that's turned cold

Cold Sweat

When I shut my eyes
you begin to shriek
You take my hand
as we're surrounded by sheep

We climb that mountain
and look to the sky
A plane passes overhead
below a train cries

We jump to the moon
unwelcome guests
When we ask for directions
the man points west

I get in your car
and you press the gas
You drive on the lake
and ask if I fish bass

Next thing I know
you pull out a gun
As you put it to your temple
you giggle, "this was fun"

Tears of Pain

Why live in reality
when the dream is what you crave
Everything is different
when nothing is the same
Help me find the answer
or aren't you that brave
Too bad I missed you
so sad you never come
Tomorrow's a new beginning
yesterday began the rain
The child full of life
crosses his hands in the grave
When I shut my eyes to go to bed
out fall tears of pain

Appease

There's a storm on the horizon
I feel it in my knees
The townsfolk talk of it's arrival
coming with the breeze
Children run for shelter
leaves fall off the trees
A woman begs forgiveness
trying to appease
It doesn't take a smart man
no need for a degree
To realize our breath will soon be
a whining little wheeze

Three Years

Three years spent building a future
that became nothing but the past
Three years of love blossoming by the day
that turned to hate so fast

Three years of knowing who I was
followed by a soul full of doubt
Three years of knowing all the answers
to not knowing what the question's about

Three years of two becoming one
in what was the imperfect fusion
Three years of total knowledge
then being hit with total confusion

Three years of beauty and bliss
done up by hurt and sorrow
Three years I wouldn't change for the world
not yesterday, today, or tomorrow

Scent of Summertime

The summer vanilla sky
brings a smile to my tears
In that brief moment of perfection
I momentarily forget my fears

I remember this world is full of greatness
and also unbelievable beauty
Perhaps seeing just the negative
isn't, after all, my sole duty

The scent of summertime
filled up my lungs
Why'd it take so long
to realize I'm still young

Now every night I ask God
for just one thing
Simply put to be positive
then I'll earn my wings

Estranged

The bridge that got burned
is the one I want to cross
So many years have passed
yet it remains the biggest loss

It's been a lifetime since we spoke
and so many things have changed
In fact the only thing that hasn't
is we continue to be estranged

I'd shout it from the rooftop
if only you'd listen
I wish I still had the ability
to make those green eyes glisten

Maybe you'll remember
the love that we shared
Until that day I'm satisfied
being the only one who cares

The Mistake

It was doomed from the beginning
a slip from the start
But you insisted on leaving
if not this town you'd depart

A spoiled little prissy
always gets her way
Even if common sense shouted
it'd only work if you'd stay

Your parents were so blind
they couldn't see their five mistakes
Daddy wrapped up in his affairs
and mommy on Prozac breaks

I was stuck with the result
of the years of mental abuse
There'd be no victory for anyone
just a game we'd all lose

Today I watch the sunset
with you no longer here
A smile fills my face
the audience begins to cheer

House of Memories

This is the house full of memories
that I never shared
Laughter, fun, and games
now tell me is that fair?

Every time I say
this visit things will change
Of course nothing ever does
I wish someone else were to blame

I removed myself from the equation
for far too long
Resulting in any chance whatsoever
of comfort being gone

I'll keep on trying
till I get it right
I almost see the sun
it's just beyond my sight

Any Day Now

It was there all along
the light I never saw
The demon let go his hold
the lion removed his claws

It didn't take much
a weekend and a prayer
To find the missing piece
a feeling that was rare

Soon everyday will see
the truck with its plow
The point I'm trying to make is
it's any day now

A retreat atop the hill
soon to be called home
Lake Michigan in the backyard
the tide begins to foam

I can't stop smiling
it's been some time since I've been excited
Onekama awaits my arrival
I've already been invited

Change of Plans

There's happiness out there
smiles to be had
Sun on the horizon
no reason to be sad

A life full of future
talks yet to share
Longing fills my inside
many people who care

A slight change of plans
the rain went away
It's time to move on
not a reason to stay

It's been so long
I'm giddy as a kid
I can fly to the moon
the cage blew it's lid

Laughter here I come
next stop a new start
Hope scented of sea
melting in my heart

It's Time

It's time to let go of old memories
and time to make some new
It's time to forget about her
and time to concentrate on you

It's time to grow up a little
and time to shine true
It's time to clean off the window
and time to change my view

It's time to alter my opinion
and time to see without my eyes
It's time to hear the conflicting tales
and time to entertain blue skies

It's time to enjoy what I have
and time to stop focusing on what I don't
It's time to wake up to myself
and time to realize I'm not alone

Kayak

The infamous last words
"it'll be okay"
I was terrified to start
predicting my dismay

I know my limitations
and this was definitely one
But she made me try it
insisting I'd have fun

So I swallowed down my fear
and gave it a try
Two seconds in
I wanted to cry

I started to shake
before I even got cold
My balance went out the window
there'd be no Olympic gold

Just as I'd foreseen
I tipped and felt I was going to die
I took on a fear
I may have lost...but I tried

Marathon

Do what you can
with what you've got
It doesn't matter if it's a little
or even if it's a lot

We all have the power
to do as we wish
Choose to fly like a bird
not sink like a fish

Live for today
and plan for tomorrow
Be full of optimism
to help erase sorrow

Never let someone else
control how you feel
That truly is an inside job
love yourself first, there's an ideal

Follow the preceding lines
and be ready for smiles
This marathon of life just began
you've got many more miles

Prelude

It's hard to articulate
the words I wish to say
Instead I write in rhyme
and express life my own way

A pen and some paper
then I'm all set
It's more therapeutic than therapy
more loyal than a pet

It's there when I need it
and even when I don't
The world is awaiting this story
soon it'll be known

Be forewarned of a tale
that may make you laugh and sometimes cry
The moral to this book
is you can do anything if you try

Sloth

I wanted to call
but I fell asleep
My head hit the pillow
before we could speak

The questions remains
what would have been?
My laziness caused a forfeit
before I had the chance to win

Sloth is a deadly sin
and I now see why
Maybe if it's not too late
we could give it one more try?

If not I understand
and thank you for the chance
Oh no I need to go lie down
the sheep are starting to dance

Hound

I fell in love with her body
and not her heart
I made the mistake of not telling her
and letting a relationship start

As hard as I tried
I couldn't turn lust into love
I could only see luscious hips
and not the white dove

Lies became accepted as truth
and the truth was nowhere to be found
I began feeling less of a man
and more of a hound

Disgust soiled my soul
But it didn't even matter
For a minute with that body
I'd put up with hours of pointless chatter

It wasn't until that day you wised up
and slammed the door in my face
That I realized my true feelings for you
and that you'd be impossible to replace

The Search

Once you give up the search
is when you'll finally find it
It won't come to you until that day...
...the day when you decide to quit

It just happens like magic
when you least expect it to
And that will be the day
when everything seems new

Colors will be brighter
and not a thing will be wrong
The air will smell of heaven
and the birds will sing your song

You'll walk with a spring in your step
and an air of confidence that'll be noticed by all
Let's hope this feeling lasts
and the maker doesn't order a recall

Growing

Today saw the day
that the storm found it's end
The strength was found inside
no help from a friend

Hopefully sunny days
are here to stay
But if I do get lost again
to return I know the way

It's been a trying half year
and the test has just begun
I've shown a different side of myself
and when challenged no longer run

I've changed so much
and keep growing more strong
I've finally found my place
and feel like I belong

Complete

I set the number
and went to work
For all your pessimism
I only could smirk

I wonder what you're thinking
as I hit my mark
It doesn't even matter
this journey's for me to embark

I can't believe this...
...for once I've finished something I started
And now it's time to sail
waters that are uncharted

Should I pass or fail
it's still up in the air
Either way I'm proud of myself
a feeling I can't compare

Printed in the United States
18096LVS00007B/26